Give Me a Moment
and I'll Change Your Life

Also by Alan Lakein

How to Get Control of Your Time and Your Life

Give Me a Moment and I'll Change Your Life

Tools for Moment Management

Alan Lakein

**Andrews McMeel
Publishing**

Kansas City

Library of Congress Cataloging-in-Publication Data

Lakein, Alan.
   Give me a moment and I'll change your life : tools for moment management / Alan Lakein.
      p.   cm.
   ISBN 0-8362-3591-6
   1. Time management—United States.   2. Success.   I. Title.
HN90.T5L33   1997
640'.43—dc21   97-16798
                                                                      CIP

ATTENTION: SCHOOLS AND BUSINESSES

Andrews McMeel books are available at quantity discounts with bulk purchase for educational, business, or sales promotional use. For information, please write to: Special Sales Department, Andrews McMeel Publishing, 4520 Main Street, Kansas City, Missouri 64111, USA.

To Cara, Diane, and David

Contents

Preface

Who wouldn't like to be happier right now? Do more work in less time? Have more leisure? Add more quality and meaning to life?

I would. (And probably you would too.)

Twenty-five years ago I thought a great deal about these questions and the result was "time management." My book *How to Get Control of Your Time and Your Life* sold over 3 million copies and defined time management as it's known in the world today.

I like to take ideas with high potential and push them in new and useful directions. After my time management concepts gained widespread acceptance, I started thinking about other ways to help people do more of what they want—and do it easier and better. The breakthrough came when I realized that:

- Moments are our key resource, the building blocks of our lives.

- Most of us do not use our moments as effectively as we could.
- We can learn to manage our moments better.

I began playing with ideas about moments and trying them out on myself and others. I became, in effect, a "moment manager." To my delight I found that moment management enabled people to do much more than they could do before. Those who tried it felt that their lives were enriched by the techniques I had developed.

Moment management does not replace time management—it complements it. Time management helps you set goals and priorities, then fill your hours and days with rewarding activities. Moment management helps ensure that the moments spent on any activity bring you the greatest possible productivity, satisfaction, and quality.

You can quickly become familiar with the techniques of moment management presented in this book. It takes effort and practice to apply them, like anything else worth doing, but each time you succeed, you are rewarded immediately. When you manage a moment well, you enjoy the benefits in that very moment.

To sense how well you're managing your moments, ask these questions and consider your responses. Do you:

- Pay attention to moments as they come along?
- Know what types of moments bring quality to your life?

- Apply management techniques, such as setting priorities and reviewing results, to your moments?
- Ensure that your moments are contributing to your goals?
- Enjoy to the fullest as many moments as possible?

Every one of your moments is an opportunity. This book shows you how to seize more of these opportunities to enrich your time and your life.

Give Me a Moment
and I'll Change Your Life

....

Chapter 1

Make moments
matter

....

You may wonder about the bold assertion I make in the title of this book. It's not that I have some wondrous power over your life. It's because moments do. Moments, when managed successfully, really can change your life. Act as if moments matter and you will be happier, get more done, have more leisure, and increase quality and meaning.

Life can be lived only moment by moment. Obviously moments matter. Yet like most people, you probably haven't paid much attention to them.

Consider some characteristics of moments. They follow one another in a constant stream. Most go by unnoticed. Some are all too brief. Others seem all too long (like the one that begins when your date calls out, "I'll be ready in a moment").

ONE MOMENT CAN CHANGE YOUR LIFE.

Some moments are so unique, so magical, that they're remembered ever after. Moreover, extraordinary as it may be, one moment can change your life.

———

Webster's Collegiate Dictionary defines a moment as a minute portion or point of time; an instant; present time, as "at the moment"; a time of excellence or conspicuousness, as "he has his moments."

These are all good definitions. Let's put them together: "A moment is a small bit of time that's happening now and is sometimes of superior quality."

Unlike a second, a moment is not a unit of time defined by the clock. You decide when it starts and when it stops. Whatever feels like a moment to you *is* a moment. As you work more consciously with moments, you'll get a clearer sense of how you want to define them for yourself.

Webster's records a surprising and interesting word relating to moments. "Momently" means from moment to moment, as "The baby watched for movement momently"; at any moment, as "The curtain will open momently"; for a moment, as "I'm borrowing the magazine momently."

You may never have heard of "momently," but Webster's indicates it's been in use for three hundred years. Now that "nanosecond," a billionth of a second, is coming into ordinary usage and "hourly" seems forever, momently may be an idea whose time has come.

———

ANY MOMENT CAN BE MANAGED.

———

"Momentous" is a wonderfully appropriate word for recognizing the power inherent in moments, even in seemingly ordinary ones. All moments share some remarkable attributes. They are free, abundant, and always there for you. Each new one offers you a fresh start. And happily for our purposes, any moment can be managed.

True, there may be feelings within a moment that make managing it difficult. We all experience sorrow, disappointment, depression, boredom, impatience, frustration, and anger. Managing the moment may require dealing with these negatives. But the same management techniques apply whether a moment contains pleasure or pain.

Most moments seem ordinary but some stand out as special. They contain an unmistakable richness, vibrancy, or bliss. I call them "quality moments." They are wonderful to experience, remember, and share with others.

We each have our own quality moments. Yours may include completing a marathon, catching a plane with only seconds to spare, watching a stirring film, or receiving unexpected praise. Another person's may include playing with a baby, going to a party, finding a long-lost friend, or feeling part of a team effort.

You have many chances every day to orchestrate quality moments that reflect your preferences. A friend did this very deliberately by the way she decorated her home. Whenever I sit in her living room, I see beauty in every direction. She says, "I've arranged this room so that no matter where you are, you see something wonderful."

———

She has created opportunities for quality moments for herself and for everyone who visits.

You too can find quality moments when you look for them. They're out there, just waiting to be appreciated. The challenge for you is to open up to, welcome, and enthusiastically embrace them as they come along.

······································

Chapter 2

Welcome
the moment

······································

Some moments call out for attention. They mark a clear, dramatic break from what went before. Imagine the moment when everyone shouts "Happy birthday" at a surprise party. Or when you learn you've just won the lottery.

Such moments are rare. Most moments require some effort to unlock their treasures. Managing a moment begins when you welcome it with an open mind and observe what it has to offer.

The process is similar in some ways to what happens when you smell a perfume. Perfumes contain many fragrances, and what you perceive changes over time. Perfumers call the fragrance you smell first the "top note." Gradually you become aware of the other scents as well. So it is with a moment. Begin with the top note that first draws your attention. Then enrich your experience by observing what else is going on.

Being aware of many notes enhances a moment. When you're about to blow out the candles on your birthday cake, what happens next? Do you get in touch with your thoughts and feelings? Do you take in your friends' faces, comments, and movements? The more details you absorb, the more memorable the moment will be.

Sometimes moments, like snowflakes, seem identical at a casual glance. But their uniqueness emerges on closer inspection. No two are alike. The more attention you give them, the more variety and richness you detect.

A KEY SKILL IN MOMENT MANAGEMENT IS SEEING A MOMENT FRESHLY.

A key skill in moment management is seeing a moment freshly. Practice this by trying a few exercises:

• *Look away.* Notice what first catches your eye, then use it to bring a new point of view to your current activity. For example, while evaluating an investment stock, you look up and see that a book on your shelf looks as if it might fall. The leaning book reminds you to look more closely at the stock's risk.

• *Use a zoom lens.* Equip yourself with an imaginary zoom lens. Start by focusing on whatever catches your attention. Then zoom in. Explore it in detail, clarifying exactly what it is you like. Next, zoom out, find something related to what you just explored, and zoom in on it. See freshly by comparing what you noticed when zooming in close and then zooming out again.

• *Change something.* Any change moves you to a new moment. If you're stuck on the wording of a product announcement, start a new file in your computer. That may be enough to clear your mind and spur you on to a creative solution.

• *Respond to whatever comes next.* Notice what you see, hear, think, or feel. React to it right now. When you realize that your chair is uncomfortable, rearrange it. If you're still uncomfortable, consider why: Your career? Your family? Something else? If nothing comes to mind, forget it. Maybe you just need to stand up and stretch.

Remember the contest rule "You have to be present to win"? When you're present, you notice fresh moments just waiting to be enjoyed. You've seen the sun set before, and you know the sun will set today—without your looking. But why let the opportunity go by? Peek outside or, better still, go outside and appreciate the wonder of this particular sunset.

. . . .

TOWARD BETTER
MOMENT MANAGEMENT

• *Do you welcome the moment?*
• *Do you look for what is unique in the moment?*
• *Do you freshen the moment?*

. . . .

....

Chapter 3

Add a plus

....

Imagine being at your favorite cousin's wedding. You have only a brief chance to talk to his new wife, and you want to make the most of it. So you tell the bride, "I'm so happy you're part of our family." In that moment you may well have added a plus to the occasion that will be cherished for years.

Adding a plus often happens spontaneously. You respond intuitively to whatever opportunity the situation offers. Sometimes, however, the moment is gone before your intuition kicks in or you figure out what plus to add. It's helpful to have in mind some pluses you can slip in:

• When at work, acknowledge a job well done, highlight the main ideas in a memo for easier processing, add a friendly note at the end of your e-mail.

• Upon arriving home, instead of taking the closest door to your apartment and going down an unpleasant corridor, walk around the front of the building. Appreciate the nice touches in the entry hall and feel good about where you live.

• Enjoy bonus humor in television comedies by looking for subtle changes from moment to moment in the characters' expressions, actions, and timing.

• Compliment people if you like what they're wearing. You derive triple pleasure from noticing what you like, sharing your appreciation, and observing their reaction.

Regularly scheduling worthwhile activities is an important time management technique for adding pluses to your life. Perhaps you've decided to play tennis three times a week. Once you're on the court, manage your moments by adding further pluses. Learn from how you and your opponent handle each serve; improve your backhand and your strategy.

Analyzing a sales or production database can be more interesting if you pay attention to the process as well as the figures. You might notice how you respond to the results, or how you resolve the issue of speed versus accuracy. Jot down ideas for improving the next analysis.

Even the most mundane situation offers add-a-plus opportunities. Use the moments it takes to cross a room to view the pictures on the wall. Swing your arms and loosen up before returning to your desk. Imagine crossing the room in a taxi.

Some pluses depend on your mood, on what feels right in the moment. When you're on vacation, basking beside the pool with a cool drink, you can add many pluses. Do you feel like closing your eyes and soaking up more sun? Starting a conversation with the person next to you? Swimming twenty laps?

Adding a plus is sometimes effective in dealing with

boredom, unhappiness, or stress. When you can bring yourself to add a pleasurable plus, you're probably well on your way out of such negative feelings.

Acknowledging the negative is often a sufficient plus to help you get back on track. Saying "We're not communicating" clears the air. Exposing the weakest part in your presentation allows you to strengthen it. Admitting an investment mistake prevents you from losing more money and frees you to invest for greater profit elsewhere.

Sometimes you can't add a plus because you're overstressed. When you feel that deadlines, problems, pressures, or other stressors are mounting up, you may be better off subtracting a minus. Stop all other work temporarily and switch to emergency measures:

1. List the stressors that are causing you discomfort.
2. Prioritize, identifying your top three sources of stress.
3. For your most severe stressors, list specific actions you can take to reduce stress right now.

Do as much as you can right away to reduce discomfort from your top stressor. Then move on to the others. Continue giving priority to stress reduction until your stress drops to an acceptable level. When it does, go back to what you were doing before the stress emergency.

If your problem isn't cumulative stress but momentary annoyance, adding a plus can remedy the situation. Say you have to make a last-minute trip to the store for a bottle of salad dressing. Instead of resenting the time spent, make the errand a relaxing transition from a hard day at work to a nice evening at home. Anticipate the pleasure of the next few hours with your dinner date. Or figure out how you're going to clean the living room in five minutes or less when you get back.

Life is like a salad bar. Each of us comes away with a plate of food assembled after our own taste at the moment. As moments go along, add the pluses that best suit your taste.

. . . .

TOWARD BETTER
MOMENT MANAGEMENT

- *What are your favorite pluses?*
- *What pluses do you add most frequently to your moments?*
- *What moments would especially benefit from added pluses?*

. . . .

Chapter 4

Add a purpose

Purpose moves moments. "Purpose" includes goals, priorities, objectives, visions, needs, and wants. Connecting with any of these energizes and motivates you to make the most of the moments you have.

LAKEIN'S TEN-WORD GUIDE TO CLARIFYING PURPOSE: LIST POSSIBILITIES; SET A-B-C PRIORITIES; DO THE A-1 PRIORITY NOW!

Adding a purpose, any purpose, gives more meaning to what you're doing. The clearer your purpose, the easier it is to add it to a passing moment. Whether you want to lower costs, increase sales, learn a new language, meet more people, or communicate better with your spouse, a well-defined purpose helps make it happen. Here's my ten-word guide to clarifying purpose simply and directly:

1. List possibilities.
2. Set A-B-C priorities.
3. Do the A-1 priority now!

Don't worry about making your list perfect. Any important omission will surface and can be added later. Revise and extend your list at least once a week.

When you've made your list, mark each item as an A, B, or C, with A's most important and C's least important. If you have many A's, designate the most important A-1, followed by A-2, A-3, A-4. Don't sweat over priorities. You can adjust them at any time.

Now you have an action plan. You've identified your A-1. If it can't be done until this evening or next month, make it your A-1 for then. Check your list again, identify a new A-1 for now, and start work on it right this moment.

TO ADD PURPOSE ASK, "WHAT DO YOU LIKE? HOW CAN YOU GET MORE RIGHT NOW?"

Sometimes listing and prioritizing are more than the moment requires. A useful shortcut to identifying purpose is to ask:

1. What do you like?
2. How can you get more right now?

In answering these questions, be quick and spontaneous. Most of the time the answers will point you to a clear purpose. But sometimes you'll have to play with them to uncover their meaning. Maybe you've just delivered an important report. You're sitting at your desk with an hour until lunch, and you're not ready to tackle your new A-1. Looking for some other purpose, you pose the first question, answer it, and then figure out how to get what you want. For example:

• *"I like apples."* (Strange first answer; after all, you're at work and you don't have an apple. But let's go on and ask the second question, "How can you get more right now?") It's not yet time for lunch. The best you can do at this moment is to imagine the burst of energy an apple gives you. This suggests a purpose: "Energize the moment."

• *"I like creativity."* Think about some task that's on your mind—a problem you have to solve, a situation you hope to improve, a brochure you need to write. Breathe . . . wait a moment . . . and another. Take note of whatever ideas flow in. Your purpose: "Feel the thrill of creativity."

• *"I like order."* Suppose you love neatening. The first draft of a letter you're working on is perceptive but sloppy. Cut unnecessary words, sharpen ideas, and make sentences short. A purpose emerges: "Keep it simple."

Whatever answers you get to these questions can help you come up with a purpose. Use the first purpose that presents itself, modify it to make it more useful, or keep going until you find one you prefer. Any purpose can motivate a moment.

When you pop the questions "What do you like? How can you get more right now?" you may get an answer like "I don't want more. I want less. Less busyness, less work, less tension." Turn this answer from a negative to a positive. Less busyness means greater peace of mind. Less work means finally catching up. Less tension means more cooperation or understanding. Once you've defined what you want more clearly, go after it in the next moment.

Another moment management tool is what I call "PSQ." Over the past hundred years, business management has shifted emphasis from productivity to satisfaction to quality. All are important. Any of them can launch you toward more purposeful moments. When you're considering what purpose to add, think PSQ—productivity, satisfaction, or quality—and choose the one that's best now.

A purpose common to many people is making money. This means different things to different people: working overtime, getting a raise, making a profit, exercising stock options. Adding a money purpose can be a powerful way to energize the moment. To enhance purpose and productivity, remind yourself what the money will buy— food on the table, a computer, or a new home. Or relate money to what it signifies—freedom, success, opportunity.

Sometimes an attitude leads to a purpose. When I do research at libraries and on the World Wide Web I'm intent on obtaining useful material fast. Since it's easy to get overwhelmed, I ruthlessly scan, skim, and skip through the data looking for quality items only. Moni-

———

toring productivity moment by moment keeps me on track.

Adding more than one purpose at a time enriches the moment further. You can do this by adding purposes of different types. Let's say you're finally getting around to a pile of dirty laundry. Count this chore as satisfying three purposes at once. It helps the family run smoothly, gives you the satisfaction of being neat and orderly, and leaves you with a gloriously empty laundry basket.

If you still haven't found a purpose to add to a moment you want to enrich, draw on one that has inspired you in the past. I'm still using these lifetime goals I created in high school: serve God, improve society, help people, have fun. If you don't have a set of purposes at hand, you can quickly create a draft:

1. Take a moment and write "Lifetime Goals" on a piece of paper. Now make your list. Write what comes to mind. Express each goal in five words or less.
2. Make a separate "Wish List" of what would make you healthier, wealthier, and wiser in both the short and long term.
3. List "Shared Goals" you have in common with others: corporate visions, family dreams, community objectives.

Merge these lists into one master list. Refer to it whenever you feel unsure about what purpose to add to the moment. Or make a game of it: Write each purpose on a separate slip of paper and put all the slips in a box. When you're lacking a sense of purpose, draw one out and add it to your next moment.

A friend often adds a self-improvement purpose. He reports, "I frequently take a few moments to celebrate my personal achievements, no matter how small. That way, managing moments enables me to achieve ever-increasing bliss." That level of commitment is rare, but it works for my friend and it may work for you too.

. . . .

TOWARD BETTER
MOMENT MANAGEMENT

- *What purposes shape your moments with family and friends?*
- *What purposes do you bring to your moments at work?*
- *What purposes deserve moments daily?*

. . . .

Chapter 5

Add an action

The only way to do your A-1 priority, or get more of what you like, is to act. You can't skip ahead and start work on your A-1 priority twenty moments from now without first living through the next nineteen moments. Welcome and use each one as it comes along. After twenty moments on your A-1 you'll probably have the momentum to keep going. ("Momentum" is another great moment word.)

MOMENTS ARE MADE FOR ACTION.

Moments are made for action. If it takes too long to think about how to act, you've lost the opportunity for action in that moment and probably in many more. Speed up the process of moving from thought to action with a technique I call "moment talk."

Moment talk uses language that keeps pace with moments as they come along. It has only a few rules. Make your sentences short (under a dozen words) and to the point (without being abrupt). Stay in the present with active verbs (I want . . . I see . . . I feel . . .).

Still not acting? Take a moment and ask Lakein's Question: "What's the best use of your time right now?" Take your first answer as your A-1. Then do it now!

When you know the best use of your time right now but are still losing precious moments to inaction, let go of your A-1 priority. Do an easy B or C instead. Everyone's entitled to a few moments off from the pressure of doing what's important but tough. Instead of worrying about the A-1:

- Do something to put a smile on your face.
- Do something to help someone else.
- Do something that must be done today.
- Do anything you can do right now.
- Complete an easy task—fast.

Or try another tack. Ask "What would happen if you did the opposite of what you're doing now?" If you're sitting, stand up. If you're standing, sit down. If you're writing a letter, imagine the answer you'd like to receive. If you're feeling out of touch, pick up the phone and call someone.

Even moments that seem destined for inaction can be saved by giving them a creative spin. While waiting on the corner for someone who's late, guess where passersby are headed, whistle a happy tune, and get to know the soles of your feet better. In a ticket line, make the people around you laugh. In a traffic jam, mentally redesign the system for getting across town.

If the traffic jam turns into gridlock, turn the motor off and bring out the gadgets. Phone in your traffic suggestions, dictate letters and memos, review faxes. If you still can't move, call rent-a-driver to look after your car while you walk to your destination.

Intuition is a great ally for acting purposefully in the moment. Tap into it by:

• *Taking a deep breath.* Feel the air enter your lungs. Hold it . . . then exhale into a fresh moment and trust your intuition.

• *Adjusting yourself mentally.* Feel a little taller, more successful, more efficient. Open up a place for your intuition to shine through.

• *Freezing . . .* Don't stir until you're clear about your next move or until something good happens. (If all else fails, unfreezing and moving will seem good.)

• *Seeing what catches your eye.* If it's the telephone, then call someone. Your shoes—polish them. The color green—stay calm.

• *Enjoying the moment.* Play with it. Having fun often makes you more receptive to intuitive answers.

If intuition can help you act, indecision can hamper you. The cure is action. Instead of wasting time because you're unable to choose between two possible ways of proceeding, toss a coin. If you find yourself hoping for a certain result, you've discovered what you really want to do. Otherwise, do what the coin dictates. Once you've started you'll know whether to keep going . . . or take a new direction. It's easier to make a course correction if you're already moving.

. . . .

TOWARD BETTER
MOMENT MANAGEMENT

- *What moves you toward action in the moment?*
- *How do you act when you're engrossed in a moment?*
- *How do you make course corrections in the midst of action?*

. . . .

Chapter 6

Add an activity

We often do more than one activity in a moment. For example, we listen to the radio while cooking. We cook on more than one burner. We talk on the phone while watching TV and making dinner.

You may find it possible to prepare dinner, mind your children, and conduct business on the telephone simultaneously without feeling overwhelmed. But think back and you'll probably recall that you once had to give each of these your full attention. Because the tasks are now familiar, you have the capacity to keep all of them going without stress.

A MOMENT MAY HOLD MORE THAN YOU THINK IT CAN.

A moment may hold more than you think it can. Consider an analogy. Suppose you're attending a neighborhood gathering in someone's home. The first people to arrive settle in the living room. As more people come in, they overflow into the dining room and kitchen.

When the meeting is about to start, the host says, "We're all friends here. But we're keeping our distance as if we were strangers. Maybe if we take a moment and chat with our neighbors we'll find we don't need as much space between us. Then more of us will be able to sit in the living room." Sure enough, after socializing a bit, people feel more comfortable with each other and move closer together. They fill the sofa and chairs and floor.

Fitting activities in a moment is also about comfort level. Your mood and energy, as well as the nature of the activities and skills involved, influence both the capacity of the moment and your ability to fill it up.

Experiment with how much you feel comfortable doing in a particular moment. If adding another activity leads to stress, forget it. Don't fall into the trap of doing more than one thing at a time just to prove how busy you are. Concentrating on only one activity may be best when you're seeking sharper focus, greater creativity, or a calmer work pace.

You may feel that certain moments are going to waste for lack of enough activity. They're easy to spot—they leave you feeling bored, restless, or trapped. Yet they also offer special opportunities because they are not being fully exploited.

Sometimes moments which seem destined to be wasted can be filled in a meaningful way. When a dozen people are gathering for a meeting, you can start talking business as soon as a few come in. Ask questions such as "What are you working on?" or "What's new in your operation?" Talk about what you've been up to. As others arrive, involve them too. Share what's already been said and ask them about their situation. Continue doing this until everyone is present. When the meeting is called to order, people are already connected and in high gear. You've added pluses to moments that could have been spent simply waiting around.

Affirmations offer another option for filling under-utilized or frustrating moments with quality. Repeating an affirmation enriches a moment and moves you toward quality activities. Try such affirmations as:

- I can enrich this moment.
- I'm aware of moments as they come.
- I can start fresh at any moment.
- I'm making moments count.
- I'm a good moment manager.
- I'm enjoying this moment.

Add other affirmations from the material in this book and from your experience with managing moments. Use whatever affirmations work best for you.

One of the toughest challenges to moment management is traveling with children. You're squeezed together into too tight a space for too long with too little to do. Opportunities to keep everyone happy exist, but you have to earn them. This is a situation ripe for adding an activity.

• *Plan ahead.* Be ready with songbooks, stories to tell, little surprises. And with acceptance and love.

• *Add fun.* Let your intuition suggest what else you can do to make the kids and you happier now. Then do it.

• *Add challenge.* Play the game of "What do you like now?" Have your children point out what they like the best as you travel along. See who can remember what they liked best when you crossed the bridge fifty miles back.

• *Add humor.* Ask the kids to look for or imagine funny things. Have them explain what they think is funny. And add a plus for yourself by finding reasons to laugh.

• *Welcome each moment,* even if that means acknowledging the negative. If the kids start fighting, play the mediator. If you call a quiet time-out, enjoy the silence. Then maybe everyone will relax, and you can pat yourself on the back.

• *Have an escape.* When it gets noisy in back, look out the window. Perhaps you're passing through some beautiful countryside. The louder and longer the noise, the more reason you have to appreciate the scenery.

• *Add purpose.* Think up moment management ideas for traveling with kids. Dream about publishing a book and using the money you make to hire a baby-sitter.

You can become more comfortable using a moment's full potential. The secret to not doing too much in the moment is to keep checking your stress level. Add or subtract activities to maintain the right balance.

. . . .

TOWARD BETTER
MOMENT MANAGEMENT

- *What activities add meaning to your moments?*
- *What activities do you add to otherwise wasted moments?*
- *Which of your activities blend well together in the same moments?*

. . . .

Chapter 7

Add an attitude

Adding an attitude to a moment is a powerful moment management technique. I use "attitude" to include position, opinion, role, mood, or outlook. It indicates a state of mind or a feeling. Different attitudes move you toward different purposes. Whether you're seeking business success, family togetherness, or self-improvement, adding an attitude to the moment can help you achieve that purpose.

Attitudes, like colored glasses, alter how you see the world. Wearing a certain outfit can make you feel special. So can putting on a certain attitude. You can change attitudes frequently or wear the same one all day.

Attitudes relate your activities to your purposes. Suppose you're working late at night on a special report. You can use an attitude to keep you going when the moments get tough. Eagerness—to learn a new skill, meet a deadline, star in tomorrow's meeting—may be the attitude with enough energy to get you through.

Or consider dressing in the morning. The attitude you bring to the task can make it an exciting part of the day. Use different attitudes for different situations. If you're rushed and distracted, focus on dressing efficiently, eliminating wasted effort. If you're self-confident, feel the power of dressing for success. If you're calm, reinforce that feeling by appreciating the color, texture, and design of your clothes. Just be sure not to enjoy the texture of your clothes so long that you're late for work.

Carpooling to work poses similar challenges. While riding, you chat, think about what you have to do that day, and notice what's around you. To enrich your moments in the car this week, try on these roles for variety:

• *People watcher.* You know everyone in the group well. Observe closely how they interact with you and with each other.

• *News announcer.* Find an item in the morning paper to share. Any topic will do. If it's an article on children's playgrounds, lead a lively discussion about your children, adult entertainment, or architecture.

• *Workout enthusiast.* When it's not your turn to drive, do isometrics.

You can also use different attitudes to make your job more rewarding. Say you work in customer service opening new accounts. The process may be the same every time, but it can be made more interesting if you vary your attitude.

The first day, your attitude is "accuracy." You strive to get all the information right the first time. When you hear the customer's name, you spell it out loud. You speak clearly as you read back the credit card number.

The second day, your attitude is "speed." You look for ways to enter data more quickly for each new account. You use the cues the customer gives you to shorten the process.

The third day, your attitude is "politeness." You put a smile in your voice. You let the customer finish talking even though you know the answer.

After these three days, you're more accurate, more efficient, and more polite. Adding attitudes to emphasize different aspects of your job makes it more stimulating. Your productivity climbs, and you're enjoying yourself more. Continue to rotate attitudes every day, or stick with one attitude for a week.

DEVELOP MOMENT-ENRICHING ATTITUDES FOR ORDINARY TASKS.

Develop moment-enriching attitudes for ordinary tasks like weeding the garden. As you work, add attitudes relating to:

• *Purpose.* Enjoy being outside in the sunshine, making your garden more attractive, and helping the flowers grow. Leave no weed unturned.

• *Efficiency.* Try chanting "ready, set, pull," or yanking the weed out cleanly with one tug. Use weeding as stretching time.

• *Achievement.* Seeing more and more weeds pile up is rewarding. When you have a lot of weeds, you have a lot of happy moments.

The techniques of adding a plus, purpose, action, activity, and attitude overlap. Yet each makes a distinct contribution to moment management. With practice you'll find it easy to select the "add" that manages a specific moment best.

. . . .

TOWARD BETTER
MOMENT MANAGEMENT

- *Do you improve your attitudes about managing moments?*
- *Do you match your attitude to the moment?*
- *Do you choose attitudes for moment management?*

. . . .

....

Chapter 8

Add a mome
(mostly at play)

....

A moment is a small bit of time. To manage it you need tools that fit in a moment. I've devised one such tool and named it "mome" (rhymes with "home"). A mome is a shortcut that shapes and enriches a moment.

A mome can come from many different sources. Clues for creating useful ones can be found almost anywhere—in a sensation, purpose, action, attitude, emotion, movement, wish, vision, or dream. A key skill in moment management is using momes to enrich your moments. The benefits are enormous.

A KEY SKILL IN MOMENT MANAGEMENT IS USING MOMES TO ENRICH YOUR MOMENTS.

One of my earliest momes relates to my love of flowers. When I was young, my mother had a garden and she filled the house with flower arrangements. Whenever I see flowers I respond to their shape, color, and pattern. My flower mome brings me quality moments.

Color is both a simple and a powerful mome. When you see bright yellow, accept it as a sunny gift from the moment and a stimulus to feel happy. Let the color of wide-open blue sky suggest limitless possibilities. Other momes based on smells, sounds, or textures can draw your attention to significant details in the moment.

Suppose you especially enjoy watching sparkling city lights, and this has become a favorite mome. You can extend pleasure by being alert for sparkling lights of any kind, such as sunlight reflecting through a prism or waves glinting at the beach. Follow the movement of the lights or daydream as you watch them. Let the lights add "sparkle" to your moment.

Momes can also be emotional states like strength, security, or serenity. You can use any feeling you've experienced or would like to experience as a mome. If your weekend at the lake, in the mountains, or by the ocean leaves you feeling healthy and centered, save the memory as a mome. Call it up when you're in need of healing energy.

A mome from your weekly card game can carry over to your job. You feel accepted as a valued player whether you win or lose. Use that feeling as a mome for emotional support when a proposal of yours is rejected or a mistake causes your project to go over budget.

A mome can also capture a specific movement, like walking with a brisk step or passing your hands slowly over a beautiful object. When you make exactly the right golf swing or move your computer mouse just so; use your muscle memory to record it. Fine-tune your mome by practicing the movement in your imagination several more times. Then, when you're on the golf course or at the computer, bring in your mome at just the right time.

Momes also help you perceive more than you might otherwise. What especially pleases you when you're at a gathering? The conversation, the setting, what everyone's wearing? Whatever adds the biggest plus for you makes an excellent mome. It defines clearly what you're looking for in a social situation. If a smile is your mome of choice, explore the wide range of smiles you encounter and the messages they convey:

- "Hello."
- "How nice to see you."
- "You're the greatest thing in my life."
- "That's funny."
- "The boss said to be nice to you."
- "Is that really my hand in the cookie jar?"

You can share momes, too. Imagine a group of people on a hike. They all walk along the same path, but each person has a different experience. While you're noticing an unusual tree, someone else is observing a rock formation. At a rest stop everyone shares their enthusiasms. After a few walks in the woods you have a set of momes that will help direct your close attention to nature's wonders. They may include:

• *Contrasts between light and dark.* Brown tree trunks against the white snow. Colorful flowers in a shady wood. Sparkling whirlpools in a muddy stream.

• *Multiples of the same pattern.* Wildflowers in a field. Leaflets on a fern frond. Stars in the night sky. Trills in a bird's song.

• *Shades of green.* Light green, dark green, evergreen. Bright green of new growth. Brownish green of sun-dried grass. Translucent green of leaves lit from behind by the sun.

Develop specific momes for important areas in your life. Draw on them frequently to enrich your moments. With momes to shape them, you'll discover how malleable moments can be.

. . . .

TOWARD BETTER
MOMENT MANAGEMENT

• *What momes are you using now?*
• *What other momes would you like to use?*
• *Which kinds of moments could benefit from momes?*

. . . .

Chapter 9

Add a mome
(mostly at work)

We've all been moved by inspiring stories of heroes overcoming enormous obstacles. You too can be a hero. When you're nervous about a crucial and tough situation, think about the "hero succeeding in spite of great odds." Use this mome when you need strength in the moment. For good luck, add the affirmation "I can do it."

Maybe you're preparing for your monthly trip to all the offices in your region. You need to come back with a solution to an important company-wide problem. You've specified your mome this time as "hero finding the treasure," and you call this to mind while going from the plane to your rental car.

Or maybe today's the day you'll finish a challenging project. You think about how you can enrich your moments when you're done. You feel like the "hero returning home after a difficult journey." You savor the relief and triumph afforded by this mome.

Sometimes momes are best expressed in question form. Theodore Levitt, my marketing professor years ago at

Harvard Business School, presented us with what I would now call a mome. Whenever we analyzed a company's position, he insisted we consider "Who is the customer and what are the customer's wants and needs?" Repeated often enough, these questions became a mome for quickly directing attention to the essential issues in a marketing case.

The questions "What do you like? How can you get more right now?" serve as an effective mome. Whatever the situation, these questions yield specific, immediately useful answers for enriching the current moment. Once you've had some practice, you can enter a moment, ask the questions, consider your answers, and come out ready to act.

Part of becoming a professional or learning a new job is to grow adept at applying the momes of the trade. Sometimes these are embodied in very familiar formulas. Salespeople follow the principle, "Make the sales calls and you'll make the sales." Postal carriers are inspired by the time-honored tradition that "the mail must get through." Doctors are guided by the Hypocratic Oath.

Training departments in organizations often design large programs to transmit the professional momes people need to perform their jobs satisfactorily. Training for moment management may well focus on momes as simple, powerful tools for getting the most from each moment.

A helpful way to organize your momes is to fit them into categories like these:

• *Old reliables.* Some favorite stores, restaurants, and foods may not make a big splash, but are consistently pleasant, so seek them out. If there's someone who greets you cheerfully when you arrive at work every day, feel good and return the greeting.

• *New discoveries.* Maybe you detect a special spark of creativity in a new employee. Or you come up with an exciting idea for decorating your store window. New discoveries, whether "cool" or "hot," contribute zing to your moments.

• *New winners.* Some of your new discoveries will turn out to be winners. Stay on top of new interests and experiences that enrich your moments, and integrate them into your life with momes.

• *Dreams of the future.* Enrich your life by answering the questions: "What moments are you dreaming about? What momes will help you achieve those dream moments?"

A friend of mine keeps a computer list of 250 momes. He adds, subtracts, and changes them to reflect his experience. I think the benefits come as much from his being aware of momes as from using particular ones.

If you like making lists, keep track for two weeks of moment-enriching shortcuts. Review and organize them, and you've got a personal list of momes you can draw on when you want to enrich a moment at home or at work.

· ·

TOWARD BETTER
MOMENT MANAGEMENT

- *Can you add more momes at work?*
- *Do you share your momes with your co-workers?*
- *Can you make your momes effective in more situations?*

· ·

....

Chapter 10

Recognize
quality moments

....

Ｈow do you recognize moments of superior quality? You know that something special is happening when:

- You're completely absorbed in what's going on.
- You're so energized you could do ten times as much, if not more.
- You notice details. You appreciate and are enriched by them.
- You feel as if you're using all your potential. You're highly creative.
- You produce results. You hear yourself say, "This is my day." Others tell you, "Good job."
- You smile and say to yourself, "This is the greatest."
- You're blissful. Everything's perfect.

STUDY CAREFULLY THE MOMENTS THAT BRING YOU THE GREATEST PLEASURE.

Study carefully the moments that bring you the greatest pleasure. This list may give you clues about where to look for your quality moments:

• *Success.* Listening to the engine purr after you've fixed your car. Completing your tax return. Beating your golf score. Resolving a personal or professional disagreement. Success is a major component of many quality moments.

• *Contrast.* When you're hot, a cool drink of water may produce a quality moment. When you're lonely, a friend's call. When you're exhausted from work, snuggling up with a good novel. Notice and enjoy the contrast between then and now.

• *Surprise.* It's very quiet. Suddenly there's a yell, "She's coming!" and everyone has a quality moment rushing to meet her. Or you're walking in the park and unexpectedly see a deer or a hummingbird. Surprise can give you a thrilling quality moment.

• *Creativity.* Solving a problem in a new way. Merging two ideas into an even better idea. Negotiating a winning situation for all involved.

• *Competence.* Entering a word in a crossword puzzle. Making the right moves in your aerobics class. Walking into a new office with a sense of self-assurance. Getting an important donation for your organization.

• *Progress.* Moving toward or attaining a long-sought goal. After years of searching for the right partner, or for a breakthrough in product development, you get your wish. Be aware of how far you've come and relish it.

• *Memories.* Childhood favorites, thoughts of old friends, nostalgia for special places. Pleasant memories are like quality moments on the shelf that you can pull out and savor here and now.

• *Relationships.* Lovers together, passion and joy. Families on vacation, going for a ride in the country, celebrating special events. Connections with associates at work. Relationships are opportunities for shared quality moments.

• *Sensory pleasures.* Seeing a pair of glittery earrings in a store window. Smelling freshly baked bread. Hearing a bird's song in the spring. Feeling the texture of grass. Your senses are the channels for many quality moments.

• *Special treats.* Receiving or giving a present. Going shopping, riding a horse or roller coaster, eating an ice cream cone. Whatever is special to you, no matter how small, enriches the moment with pleasure.

A quality moment can include purposes, actions, and other momes that combine to produce a richness that is exhilarating. Say you've just hung up the phone with a customer after making a big sale. You feel wonderful about connecting with your purposes of making money, helping your family, and doing a good job.

You use your "conquering hero" mome to savor the moment. You add action by phoning a prospect for a similar product, then stopping at a co-worker's desk to share the good news. In this case you have not only recognized a quality moment but have also seized the opportunity to make a rich moment even richer.

TOWARD BETTER
MOMENT MANAGEMENT

- *What characterizes quality moments for you?*
- *What are your favorite quality moments?*
- *What situations generate the most quality moments for you?*

······································

Chapter 11

Search for quality

······································

Sometimes quality moments seem to be a gift from the universe. At other times they seem to happen only after careful preparation and hard work. Search and you'll find more of them, even when you least expect them. The potential for quality moments is everywhere.

THE POTENTIAL FOR QUALITY MOMENTS IS EVERYWHERE.

Much of life is made up of moments that are routine, repetitive, unexciting, even boring. Wouldn't it be nice if quality moments came along more or less automatically in the course of brushing your teeth or riding the commuter train? Unfortunately, they don't. Not all moments are magic ones. Still, you can modify many routines to include quality moments.

If doing a few stretching exercises each morning leaves you with a glow of good health, be sure you awaken early enough to fit them in before leaving for work.

Extend this mome to a new setting by stretching again during your afternoon coffee break.

Stretch your imagination as well, and you'll be able to insert your wildest dreams into ordinary moments. Suppose you've always wanted to:

• *Climb a mountain.* Next time you're walking home from the bus, take the route straight up the hill and pretend you're ascending Mount Everest.

• *Build your dream house.* Next time you're washing the car, visualize it in front of your very own castle.

• *Be a duck.* Next time you're caught in a pouring rain struggling to hail a taxi, realize you're still fine even though you're soaking wet.

INCLUDE QUALITY MOMENTS IN ACTIVITIES YOU DO FREQUENTLY.

Include quality moments in activities you do frequently. Ask "What do you like? How can you get more?" Make lists of what you like in situations that come up often. Then, once you're clear about what you like, look for opportunities to get more.

Your list might include these entries. Office—helping co-workers, having friendly people around. Cafeteria line —being polite, smelling the food, dreaming of having a serving of each of your favorites. Elevator—sensing the thrill of gravity as the car speeds up and slows down; preparing yourself to do the A-1 priority when you arrive at your floor.

Be creative about how you approach even the most mindless task, like carrying your paperwork to and from the office. Can you extract a quality moment by focusing on the briefcase you carry? Was it a gift from someone special? Does it make you feel organized and efficient? Do you want to buy different cases to match your purposes or outfits?

Even an unavoidable task can reveal pluses if you search for them. Each time you write a check, take a moment to be thankful you have money in the bank to cover it.

One of the best ways to find quality while doing a routine task is to pause now and then. Spontaneous breaks are fine; just be sure you don't let them cut too much into your work time. Planned breaks at regular intervals are sometimes even better. Take a moment's break every five to twenty minutes. (Experiment with what interval works best for you.) Set a timer to remind you when to pause. Stand up, drink some water, look out the window, glance at the pictures on your desk.

Pausing to breathe deliberately and consciously is a simple yet effective break. Draw a slow, deep breath. Let it move you into a fresh moment. Return to your task with a sense of well-being, determination, or whatever is needed to move ahead.

A break between two activities provides a good opportunity for a quality moment. I work out regularly in a gym. Before lifting weights I stretch to relax my muscles. Then I use the moments walking to the weight room to prepare myself mentally for rigorous exercise. The shift from relaxation to exertion is always a quality moment.

The zooming technique, a favorite of mine, makes it possible to spot quality moments that might otherwise be missed. Imagine you're looking through a zoom lens. Zoom in on whatever attracts you right now. Then use your lens in one of these ways:

• *Stay zoomed in close and fully absorb the detail.* (Like picking out the French horn while listening to a symphony.)

• *Zoom out a bit.* Take in a little wider view and see how the detail you zoomed in on relates to what's around it. (Like noticing a dab of bright red color in an otherwise somber painting, then finding subtle shades of red elsewhere in the picture.)

• *Zoom far out.* After your close-in look, check for something similar to enjoy in a much wider frame. (Like appreciating a ballerina's movements, then noting how they're echoed by the whole ballet corps as well as by the response of the audience.)

Try the zoom lens technique in a team meeting. "Momently" zoom in on a detail in the discussion. As a colleague is talking, notice moment by moment when others change their expressions. Are people becoming distracted? Are they sitting up more alertly? Are they taking sides? When positive change occurs in the team, point it out. Acknowledging this change may produce a quality moment for everyone.

You can also increase your chances of finding quality moments by searching in the right places. If you like exciting action, go to a football game and keep your eyes on the quarterback. If you like rubbing elbows with celebrities, wait in front of their favorite restaurants. If you like dancing, but are stuck at home washing dishes, decide you're in the right place anyway. Tap your feet, swing your hips, and hum a tune while you're at the sink. Feel the rhythm and grace of the dance as you handle the plates and glasses.

Add more quality to at least one routine a week. You'll be surprised how many extraordinary moments can be found in even the most ordinary circumstances.

. . . .

TOWARD BETTER
MOMENT MANAGEMENT

- *Do you actively look for quality moments?*
- *What quality moments do you include in your daily routines?*
- *What can you do to upgrade more moments to quality?*

. . . .

··

Chapter 12

Examine attitudes toward quality

··

When you travel, you can sit back and wait for adventure to come to you. But if you want more quality moments, you do better to take an assertive attitude and go out looking for them.

Create your own moment management success story—with moments experienced and savored to the fullest. Do this by:

- Choosing to live a quality life.
- Expecting more quality moments to come your way.
- Enjoying the excitement that such moments offer.

Affirmations are one of the best ways of reminding yourself that you expect and deserve quality. When you awake in the morning, give yourself a pep talk. Try "Quality moments are out there today. Don't pass them by. Let them enrich you." Put a reminder by each phone so that whenever you're on hold, you remember to search for an opportunity to let the moment enrich you. Put affirmations on your bulletin board or computer so you'll see them often.

Use a "hat trick" to realize the quality in a moment. Suppose you're standing on the corner, watching people go by. You see someone wearing a hat of a particular color and, since you love hats of that color, you count it as a quality moment. If hats of that color rarely show up, your quality moments will be few and far between.

But what if you include hats of a second color in your definition of a quality moment? Having increased your chances, you'll enjoy more quality moments. Similarly, you may like a particular hairstyle, walk, or smile. Each one alone may produce a few quality moments, but combine them and soon you have many more. A trick that may seem trivial when applied to hats may be profound when applied to people, ideas, or events.

What do you do when you're experiencing a moment that doesn't quite deserve the "quality" label? Don't toss it aside. See if you can find enough additional quality to elevate it to full quality status. How?

• *Be generous.* Give it the benefit of the doubt. "The photography contest was a good learning experience even though I'm disappointed at not winning first prize."

• *Take the high road.* "This is a great day for sight-seeing, even though I'm lost and this street doesn't seem to be on the map."

• *Reassess it.* "This textbook is boring, but it will help me finish the training course and get my certificate."

Many of us have ready-made excuses for not getting the most out of a moment. Low energy is a common one. If you expect quality moments only when your energy is high, you may be missing some good opportunities. Lack of energy doesn't scare them away. On the contrary, when you're slowed down, opportunities may surface that might otherwise not have been exposed.

Maybe you're too busy to take time for quality moments—another common excuse. Faced with an opportunity for a special moment, you may feel pulled away by some other demand. Perhaps you think to yourself, "This could be great, but I'm supposed to be somewhere else now." Think again. Rejecting a quality moment takes time and energy. Pausing to embrace it, despite how busy you are, may make it easier for you to respond efficiently to the pressing demand.

A KEY SKILL IN MOMENT MANAGEMENT IS LETTING THE MOMENT ENRICH YOU.

A key skill in moment management is letting the moment enrich you. Many people put limits on their happiness by worrying, consciously or unconsciously, that something terrible might happen if they're too happy. The affirmation "I deserve quality moments" may open the door for you to let in more joy. The more you can allow the moment to enrich you, the greater will be your PSQ.

Although increasing your ability to absorb happiness may be the most difficult challenge of all, it may have the biggest payoff. True, too much of a good thing, like too many chocolate chip cookies, can be bad. But in many situations, removing self-imposed limitations can dramatically improve the quality of your life. The next time you suspect you're cutting short a quality moment, resist the temptation. Look around and, if everything seems safe, go ahead and enjoy it to the fullest.

. . . .

TOWARD BETTER
MOMENT MANAGEMENT

- *How are you limiting quality moments for yourself?*
- *How can you be open to more quality moments?*
- *What attitudes encourage quality moments?*

. . . .

··

Chapter 13

Cultivate
quality moments

··

Even a single quality moment can change your life. Some people call this a "magic moment." Maybe there's an element of good fortune in when a particular one comes along, but you can cultivate luck, too. Quality moments, like trees, children, and relationships, grow on their own. But your nurturing can make a big difference.

Your parents glow with happiness when you arrive on their anniversary with yellow roses just like those outside the front door when you were growing up. (You may not believe this, but a friend once sent 500 roses to his mother on her birthday.) Nostalgia, love, gratitude, and pleasure combine to make a perfect moment.

When you're preparing a special dinner for two, build quality into the occasion by anticipating every step. As you bring out the candles, think about how they will make the moment more romantic. Do the same as you arrange the flowers, select the music, and prepare each dish. Continue tuning up for the big moment by fluffing a pillow and putting an interesting book on the coffee table. Check your outfit one more time, then enjoy the evening.

The technique of cultivating quality moments works well for me when I'm at a party with a room full of strangers. I find adventure and satisfaction in sharing a quality moment with as many different people as possible. I get so wrapped up in going after quality moments that I forget to worry about not knowing anyone.

CULTIVATING QUALITY IS ABOUT KNOWING WHAT YOU LIKE AND GOING AFTER IT.

Cultivating quality is about knowing what you like and going after it. Let your preferences in various categories lead you to quality moments:

• *People.* Celebrities, spiritual leaders, mentors, best friends, lovers, co-workers.

• *Places.* Your honeymoon spot. The executive dining room. The breathtaking view of your favorite city as your plane nears the airport.

• *Situations.* When you hear "yes" to borrowing the car, getting the job, or obtaining last-minute tickets to a hit show. When you hear "I love you," "You're wonderful," or "Thanks for doing such a great job." When your grandchild laughs.

Some events abound in shared quality moments. Parties, parades, and political victories let many people join together in celebration. Sports do also, providing such crowd-pleasing moments as home runs, goals, and baskets.

Rock concerts are multimedia efforts to create quality moments. They're not only music but also crowds, costumes, movement, clapping, cheering, spotlights, colors. A wealth of input. A wealth of opportunities for shared enthusiasm.

Many festivals and rituals around the globe are designed to be group experiences of quality moments. Holiday celebrations are a joyous blending of tradition and spontaneity in which all participate.

ART IS A COLLECTION OF QUALITY MOMENTS FROZEN IN TIME AND SPACE.

Art is born of inspired moments captured by a painter, sculptor, composer, or writer, perhaps hundreds or even thousands of years ago. The result is a collection of quality moments frozen in time and space. A great work of art transmits the force of these inspired moments to viewers, listeners, and readers.

Quality moments include a spiritual dimension for many people. They feel a connection with life, nature, God, a greater Self, or the whole of creation. In this dimension even ordinary moments transcend everyday existence and feed the soul. At its most intense, a moment can become a revelation that brings about a fundamental shift in values and concepts. Such a moment is truly transformative.

. . . .

TOWARD BETTER
MOMENT MANAGEMENT

- *What people lead you to quality moments?*
- *What places lead you to quality moments?*
- *What situations lead you to quality moments?*

. . . .

······································

Chapter 14

Replay
quality moments

······································

You can relive a quality moment by remembering it in the present. Experienced anew, it can be even better than the original, its richness multiplied by the recollection of pleasure. Each time you replay a quality moment in your mind, you can explore new angles or linger on favorite details.

If you are a dedicated bird-watcher, for example, you probably keep a yearly list as well as a life list of all the bird species you've seen. You're replaying quality moments when you review your lists. Recalling the circumstances surrounding a particular sighting allows you to relive the original experience.

You can do the same by recalling other favorite quality moments. Souvenirs from your travels, photos of friends and relatives, and treasures from your past trigger recollections of moments rich in quality. Is it possible to get enjoyment again and again from the same moments? Of course—just watch how excited your child is whenever you come to the "good" part of a story that you've already read fifty times.

I get the same kind of excitement when listening to one of my favorite pieces of classical music. Toward the end there's a beautiful ten-second passage that provides quality moments full of anticipation and enjoyment.

SPEND MORE TIME ON THE A'S. DO FEWER C'S.

I listen to music for hours on end (and am listening while writing this now). Each day I play whatever I'm in the mood for. My listening follows the principle, "Spend more time on the A's. Do fewer C's." I label my favorites as A's and listen to them at least once a month. Sometimes I play my A-1, A-2, and A-3 every day. The B's get a hearing every couple of months, and the C's about once a year to provide variety. Scheduling my listening ensures that favorites—old and new—get their turn.

When scheduling, be sure to allow enough time for what you like and schedule your best A's frequently. This takes care of what you've already defined as favorites. How do you add new A's to your repertoire? Follow your bliss. What feels good is an excellent guide to new A's.

Another way is by getting to like more of what you find. For example, pop music's Top Forty includes lively songs, quiet songs, love songs, rap, loud beats, soloists, and groups. Appreciating all of these gives you more quality moments.

A few years ago, I drove back and forth between Northern and Southern California every month. Since I enjoy popular music, I took along the Top Ten popular albums. When I first listened to some new releases, I didn't like them. But after a couple of replays I began to appreciate them. Without exception, I ended up enthusiastic about every one.

How is this possible? A producer of some of these albums once told me: "Any song that makes the Top Forty must be good music from some point of view. The top ones always have something extra special. To like it, find the point of view that makes it work."

So I approach a popular song by looking for what's special about it. Attentive listening lets the music tell its story. At first a song may turn me off, but after playing it several times, I always feel good about it. Each replay brings more pleasure.

With so many rewards coming from quality moments, it's worth being aggressive in hunting for them. Stay on the trail of positive feelings like a bloodhound. Develop a nose for them. When you come upon them, fix them in your memory the way a bloodhound memorizes a scent. These are then momes available to lead you to many more quality moments.

. . . .

TOWARD BETTER
MOMENT MANAGEMENT

- *What quality moments do you schedule during each day?*
- *What quality moments do you want to replay at least monthly?*
- *How can you expand your range of quality moments?*

. . . .

Chapter 15

Make the
moment yours

Every moment is unique. With practice, you can tune into that uniqueness. Once you've embraced a moment and made it yours, you're rewarded instantly.

But don't expect to manage every moment. Be satisfied at first with paying full attention to a few each day. Start slowly and build on your successes.

- Watch a moment closely as it evolves.
- Enrich it when you see an opportunity.
- Be receptive to the enrichment that it offers you.

Do a little analysis afterward. You might even want to keep a moment management journal reviewing what you did, what you might have done, and what the results were. Then take the rest of the day off. Manage a few more moments tomorrow.

LAKEIN'S NINE-WORD GUIDE TO MOMENT MANAGEMENT: ENRICH THE MOMENT AND LET THE MOMENT ENRICH YOU.

This book contains many tools to help you manage a moment successfully for PSQ (productivity, satisfaction, and quality). Underlying them all is a single purpose, attitude, and guide to action: "Enrich the moment and let the moment enrich you." These nine words are my A-1 message to you about how to be a skillful moment manager. You can think of it as both a summary of the techniques in this book and a powerful mome for daily moment management.

As moment follows moment, you'll have many opportunities to recall and use this mome. Enriching one moment and reaping its rewards make you better able to manage the next. It won't be many days before you'll be managing so successfully and living so fully that the results will show in all areas of your life.

When you give more to a moment, it gives more to you. Live more quality moments and you'll experience more bliss. At times this bliss may carry you to a sphere beyond the moment. For me this is a place of peaceful wonder even in the midst of busy activity—a place beyond words and even beyond time that some would call spiritual.

Happily, you don't have to travel to the spheres to know this bliss. All you have to do is let this very moment be a rewarding experience. If you notice, shape, and appreciate your moments, the bliss takes care of itself.

. . . .

TOWARD BETTER
MOMENT MANAGEMENT

- *Look over all the questions in the previous "Toward better moment management" boxes.*
- *Select a few areas that you want to improve, and work on them every day for a month.*
- *Once a month identify areas for further improvement, and continue your efforts to be a better moment manager.*

. . . .

Appendix:
Are you managing your moments?

1. Do you manage your moments as you do other valuable, scarce resources?

2. Do you act as if moments matter?

3. Do you enjoy playing with moments?

4. Do you cultivate quality moments?

5. Do you look for opportunities to relive quality moments?

6. Do you include quality moments in routine tasks?

7. Do you enhance moments with positive attitudes?

8. Do you use the moment to achieve your goals, priorities, objectives, and dreams?

9. Do you seize the moment?

10. Do you enrich the moment and let it enrich you?